Versos sencillos

Simple Verses

José Martí

Translated, with an Introduction,
by Manuel A. Tellechea

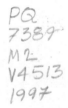

D0043338

Recovering the U.S. Hispanic Literary Heritage
Arte Público Press
Houston, Texas
1997

This volume is made possible through a generous grant from the Rockefeller Foundation.

Recovering the past, creating the future

Arte Público Press
University of Houston
Houston, Texas 77204-2174

Cover illustration by Raymond Ortiz Godfrey
Cover design by Mark Piñón

Martí, José, 1853-1895.
  [Versos sencillos. English & Spanish]
  Versos sencillos = Simple verses / by José Martí ;
translated by Manuel A. Tellechea.
    p.   cm. — (Recovering the U.S. Hispanic Literary
Heritage Series)
    Summary: A collection of poems that constitutes a
spiritual autobiography of José Martí, the renowned Cuban
poet, philosopher, and patriot.
    ISBN 1-55885-218-2 (cloth). — ISBN 1-55885-204-2
(pbk. : alk. paper)
    [1. Cuban poetry. 2. Spanish language materials—
Bilingual.] I. Tellechea, Manuel A. II. Title. III. Series:
Recovering the U.S. Hispanic Heritage Project publication.
PQ7389.M2V4513   1997
861—dc21   97-22189
                                                               CIP
                                                               AC

The paper used in this publication meets the requirements of the American National Standard for Permanence of Paper for Printed Library Materials Z39.48-1984.

9 0 1 2 3 4 5 6 7   10 9 8 7 6 5 4 3 2

A Manuel Mercado, de México.
A Enrique Estrázulas, del Uruguay.

To Manuel Mercado, of Mexico.
To Enrique Estrázulas, of Uruguay.

Introduction

I remember the first time I read *Versos sencillos*. I was five or six at the time, but knew even then that to commune with superior beings one must ascend to their heights; and so, laboriously, I climbed the ladder in the garage, and sitting atop it, began to declaim Martí's verses, which were a primer of sorts for me.

I undertook to translate Martí at the age of thirteen, and worked, more or less continuously, for 20 years on the project. When I finally finished the translation I found myself close to Martí's age when he had composed it; but farther from him than when I was a boy, for now no ladder was high enough—not even the mountain of papers I had accumulated—to reach his boundless glory. I hope, however, that this translation may be the first rung on the ladder that will bring many closer to José Martí, who was and remains one of the world's essential men.

José Julián Martí Pérez was born in Havana, Cuba on January 28, 1853. The man who would someday become the national hero and cultural icon of the Cuban nation was the son of a Spanish soldier, Mariano Martí Navarro (verse XLI of *Versos sencillos*), and a Canary Islander, Leonor Pérez Cabrera (verse XXVII), who arrived on the island in practically the last wave of colonial emigration. Yet no man was ever more attached from birth to his native land or more certain that their destinies were bound and inextricable: Lacking Cuban roots himself—racially and culturally distinct from his countrymen—Martí would nonetheless forge a common identity for all Cubans, become the champion of a doubly-enslaved race (verse XXX), and unite in common cause the disparate forces that waged the definitive struggle against Spanish rule in Cuba. By laying the foundation for Cuba's independence from Spain, Martí effectively ended the era of colonialism begun by Columbus and completed the work of hemispheric liberation initiated by Bolívar. His death in battle at age 42 on May 19, 1895 may well be regarded as the beginning of Latin America's modern era. The most respected political thinker and exponent of democracy in the history of Latin America, Martí was also its first truly great poet and writer.

Martí's patriotic and literary vocation were born together. At age 15, shortly after the outbreak of The Ten Years' War for Cuban independence in 1868, Martí had his first encounter with Spanish despotism when the local militia, known as the "Volunteers," responded to cheers for independence at the Villanueva Theatre by opening fire on the unarmed crowd (verse XXVII). In the wake of this incident, Martí's teacher and mentor, the poet Rafael María de Mendive, who was known to be sympathetic to the rebel cause, was arrested and subsequently deported to Spain. The day after the massacre Martí published in the clandestine *La Patria Libre* his precocious play, *Abdala*, whose adolescent hero dies defending his homeland from a foreign invader; and less than a month later, his sonnet "¡10 de Octubre!" appeared in *El Siboney*, a student newspaper. Arrested for treason for championing the cause of Cuban independence, and for chastising in a letter a schoolmate who had enlisted in the criminal volunteer militia, Martí was sentenced by a military tribunal to six years at hard labor at the San Lázaro Quarry. Martí was 16 when he entered prison. Outfitted with an iron waist-chain and leg shackles that were never removed during his incarceration, Martí would bear for the rest of his life bloody stigmata where the iron had dug into his flesh.

Through an influential friend, Martí's parents succeeded in having their ailing son transferred to the Isle of Pines and finally got his sentence commuted to deportation to Spain in 1871. There Martí attended the Universities of Madrid and Saragossa, and published *El presidio político en Cuba* (1871), which denounced the inhuman treatment of political prisoners in Cuban jails; and *La República española ante la Revolución cubana* (1873), which appealed in vain to the newly founded Spanish Republic to recognize that Cubans had the same right to self-determination as Spaniards did. Despite his brutal treatment at the hands of the agents of Spanish colonialism, Martí recalled fondly his years in Spain as the formative ones of his life and even hailed the courage of the martyrs who died to end Spain's legacy of superstition and intolerance (verse VII).

After being examined and approved for degrees in law, philosophy and the humanities, Martí, still under an order of deportation, evaded Spanish surveillance and briefly stopped at Paris, where he met Victor Hugo, whose *Mes Fils* he translated. From Paris he sailed to Mexico by way of Southampton and New York, and was finally reunited with his destitute family in 1875. Martí joined the staff of the *Revista Universal*, and his play *Amor con amor se paga* (1875) was performed at the Teatro Principal. In Mexico Martí lost the favorite of his seven sisters, Mariana Matilde (verse VI); and became engaged to his future wife, the daughter of a wealthy Cuban émigré, Carmen Zayas Bazán (verses XVIII, XX, XXXV and XXXVII). There he also met the lawyer Manuel Mercado, who became his steadfast friend and lifelong confidante (*Versos sencillos* is co-dedicated to him).

Of Mexico Martí said that "next to his own it was the country he loved most." But he would not be allowed to remain there, either. The sudden rise of Porfirio Díaz compelled his departure. Risking certain imprisonment if detected, Martí arrived clandestinely in Havana in January 1877 under the pseudonym "Julián Pérez." Less than two months later Martí was in Guatemala, where he taught at the normal school run by the Cuban José María Izaguirre and was named to the faculty of the university. In the year he was in Guatemala, Martí undertook at the government's request a review of the country's new legal statutes, and on his own initiative wrote and published his classic history of Guatemala. But it was all unavailing: When his friend Izaguirre was unjustly dismissed from his post, Martí renounced his own and left the country.

Of his stay in Guatemala, Martí cherished always the memory of María García Granados, whose innocent love he renounced, only to realize many years after her death that she was also his true love (verse IX).

Availing himself of the general amnesty decreed by Spain at the conclusion of The Ten Years' War in 1878, Martí returned to Havana with his wife Carmen, who, on November 22, gave birth to his only child, José Francisco Martí Zayas Bazán (verses 1:10 and XXXI).

Denied by the government a license to practice law, Martí worked as a legal clerk while engaged in helping to organize a new uprising on the island under the direction of the Comité Revolucionario Cubano, based in New York. On the resumption of hostilities on the island, and without charges being presented against him, Martí was once more banished to Spain and managed again to escape across the Pyrenees, arriving in New York on January 3, 1880, bereft of his closest affections, the infant son he adored and a wife who struggled in vain to understand an altruism which seemed to her at times not only to supersede his family but to exclude it.

Without assured means of support in a foreign land, Martí took lodgings in a boarding house owned and run by two Cuban émigrés, Manuel Mantilla and his wife Carmen. Unable at first to find adequate employment, and trailed round-the-clock by Pinkerton agents hired by the Spanish consul, Martí resumed immediately his revolutionary activity, and was named spokesman and then interim-president of the Comité Revolucionario Cubano. Engaged as an art critic for *The Hour* and *The Sun,* whose legendary editor, Charles A. Dana, regarded him as "a man of genius," Martí was finally able to send for his family from Cuba. His wife, however, was not accustomed to the rigors demanded of all new immigrants. Barely a week after the failure of the most recent uprising on the island, having lost all hope of convincing Martí to return with her to Cuba and what would have been at best an uncertain future, she left with their son in November 1880. Later, she consented to rejoin her husband, only to abandon their home again, this time with the connivance of the Spanish consul in New York.

In January 1881, with nothing to hold him in New York anymore, Martí sailed for Venezuela, where he was to remain six months: long enough for him to found the *Revista Venezolana,* the first modern journal of arts and opinion in Latin America, and write *Ismaelillo,* which contains the most beautiful poetry ever dedicated by a father to his son. While in Venezuela, Martí met and befriended shortly before his death Cecilio Acosta, the country's leading democrat, then under house arrest by the "Illustrious Regenerator," as the dictator General Guzmán Blanco was formally known. Martí's obituary of Acosta was both an appreciation of his life and a vindication of the democratic principles for which he lived. When Martí refused to dedicate a similar panegyric to

Guzmán Blanco, an order of expulsion was decreed against him.

Martí attempted to settle in Venezuela, as he had previously in Mexico and Guatemala; but his unequivocal opposition to the excesses of arbitrary rule inevitably brought him into conflict with the leaders of these countries, who found it impossible to purchase his praise or his silence. His outspokenness in the face of injustice won him, however, the admiration of the best and most representative men of every land where he lived.

Martí returned in August 1881 to New York, where he was to remain for the last 14 years of his life. Here he found at last the freedom which everywhere eluded him and the stable family life which he always craved. After Mantilla's death, Martí became a surrogate father to the four children of Carmen Miyares, and in her found a constant companion who did not resent his love of Cuba but shared it (verse IV).

In the United States, Martí was to launch two revolutions: one in the sphere of letters and another in that of human affairs. The literary revolution began with the publication in 1882 of *Ismaelillo*, which many critics regard as the birth of Modernism in Spanish poetry. His novel *Amistad funesta*, serialized in 1885, was the first to introduce ideas in a novel of manners. *La Edad de Oro* (1889) pioneered the genre of children's literature in Latin America and remains its outstanding example. Martí's greatest influence, however, was exerted in journalism, which he elevated to a literary craft and placed at the service of humanity.

More than any other man Martí is credited with having acquainted the Latin two-thirds of the Western Hemisphere with the other third. He did this through bi-weekly columns published over a decade in Mexico's *El Partido Liberal* and *La Nación* of Buenos Aires, which were reprinted in a score of newspapers throughout Latin America, making Martí the first internationally syndicated political commentator. Martí had one major subject: the United States, to which five of the 28 volumes of his *Obras completas* are devoted. Martí introduced Emerson and Whitman to the Hispanic world and was the first and most influential exponent of hemispheric transculturation; indeed, he shaped Latin America's view of the United States much as de Tocqueville did Europe's. Martí also dissected U.S. politics and warned of the perils which it held for Latin America in the heyday of jingoism. He did not conceal the faults inherent in the American system of government, and he railed against them with all the force of a sympathizer, but he deplored the faults, not the system, which he always regarded as the paramount achievement of man as a social animal.

As his fame and influence spread in Latin America, Martí was appointed by Argentina and Paraguay to head their respective consulates in New York. That same year Martí was also named by Uruguay as its representative to the International American Monetary Conference, in Washington, where he was instrumental in defeating a U.S. plan to gain control of the economies of Latin America by placing silver on a par with gold as the regional standard of exchange—a plan inspired by the recent discovery of mass silver deposits in the West.

Exhausted by work in that "winter of despair" when the sovereignty of the nations of Latin America and the future of Cuba seemed to hang in the balance, and suffering from a pulmonary disorder which may have been tuberculosis, Martí was advised by his doctor to seek an "air cure" in the Catskill Mountains of upstate New York. Finding it impossible to be idle, Martí composed during his convalescence the greater part of the *Versos sencillos*, a universal monument of Hispanic-American culture which, if all his other works were lost, would alone assure him the same place in its literary pantheon.

Versos sencillos is the poetical autobiography of Martí's soul: Each poem captures an experience, a sensation, or a moment which shaped the poet and the man. For more than 100 years, these poems have been part of the life of an island and a continent: Martí's reformulation of the Golden Rule, "La rosa blanca" (verse XXXIX), is perhaps the most anthologized poem in Latin America and the first most children are taught in school; "La niña de Guatemala" (verse IX), the best and most famous love poem in Hispanic literature; "La bailarina española" (verse X), the first Spanish poem to capture in words the rhythm of dance; "Yo tengo un amigo muerto" (verse VIII), the first Surrealist poem in the language; and the patriotic verse (XXIII, XXV, XLV), the only expression of love of country without bombast or chauvinism to be found in the poetry of his time. But *Versos sencillos* is more than its individual poems, however dazzling. The poet and the warrior, the troubadour and the philosopher, the lawgiver and the truthseeker, the enraptured and the disenchanted lover, the defender of poetry and its reformer, the genius and the pure man, all alternate in *Versos sencillos* in a symphony as perfectly modulated as the life it represents. Martí is the universal man: Only his capacity for sacrifice is limitless and his principles unshakable.

On December 13, 1890, Martí read from the manuscript of *Versos sencillos* at a soirée in honor of Francisco Chacón Calderón held in the home of Carmen Miyares, at 361 West 58th Street, in New York City. *Versos sencillos* would be published in October 1891 by Louis Weiss & Co. of New York. It was the last of his books to appear in his lifetime: His "hirsute" *Versos libres*, alluded to in the prologue to *Versos sencillos*, would be published posthumously. For what remained of his life, Martí took with him copies of *Versos sen-*

cillos wherever he traveled to give to old and new friends: a part of himself, as it were, which he left with every worthy man, woman and child he met.

Of Martí as a poet only one thing needs still to be said: From the death of Whitman in 1892 to his own death in 1895, Martí was the greatest poet, Anglo or Hispanic, in the United States at that time, a fact not known by many then or now. But since he wrote and published almost all his books in this country, in concert with, and often ahead of, the progress of American culture and literature, it is impossible not to consider him also a part of the U.S. literary heritage and certainly the greatest Hispanic contributor to it.

Throughout this period of literary creation and renovation, Martí never abandoned the quest for Cuban independence, which remained the focus of his life to which all his other activities contributed and were subordinate. Martí wrote that "man needs poetry to live as he does light and air;" and *Versos sencillos* confirmed that the poet needs it more than any other man (verse XLVI). But Martí was not an esthete who believed in art for art's sake. The greatest artist in Latin American history also wrote: "In times of revolution, everything must go in the fire, even art, to feed the flames."

In 1884, Martí was asked by the two outstanding military leaders of The Ten Years' War, generals Máximo Gómez and Antonio Maceo, to spearhead a campaign in Latin America to raise funds for a new uprising on the island; but owing to differences arising from what role if any the military should play in the conduct of civic affairs, and fearing that the generals (who blamed the divisive government of the Republic-in-Arms for the failure of the last war) wanted to establish a military dictatorship, he excluded himself from their premature plan, recognizing that the generals were better than their plan. The failure of the Gómez-Maceo Plan and other aborted schemes convinced

Martí that the country needed time to heal from the defeatism and personal antipathies fostered by the failure of Cuban arms in the last war.

By 1891, Martí discerned the right conditions existed to bring his "necessary war" to Cuba—"necessary" not only to secure independence, but to prevent the United States from realizing its historic potential to annex Cuba either through purchase or by force. Martí had fought the rising tide of American imperialism as a diplomat and journalist: Now he would do so as a soldier.

On April 5, 1892, at a meeting of the various Cuban patriotic clubs in Key West, Martí proposed the creation of the Cuban Revolutionary Party "to unite in purpose and sufficient strength all the elements needed to accelerate, through a revolutionary organization of democratic spirit and methods, the establishment of a republic where every citizen, Cuban or Spaniard, white or black, American or European, may enjoy in work and peace the full rights of man." The *Bases* and *Estatutos* of the party, drafted by Martí, were submitted to a general vote and unanimously approved; and Martí was elected without opposition the Delegate (or leader) of the Cuban Revolutionary Party. With only the force of his personality and the power of his oratory, Martí united a fractured exile community and gave new life to what for many had become a lost cause.

Though often gravely ill, poisoned on one occasion and nearly assassinated on another by Spanish agents, his every movement monitored by Pinkerton detectives and U.S. Customs inspectors, Martí would make over the next three years innumerable trips throughout the United States and Latin America to sustain the resolve of his fellow exiles and raise the funds necessary to equip ships and purchase armaments. He also edited and largely wrote *Patria*, the organ of the party.

Introduction

When the "Fernandina" expedition, the culmination of all his revolutionary work, was betrayed and its ships and their contents seized by the U.S. government in January 1895, Martí compressed into a few weeks the labor of years and organized another which was not detected. On January 29, Martí signed the order for hostilities to commence on the island; and two days later, sailed for the Dominican Republic to join General Máximo Gómez, who, putting aside past differences, had accepted supreme military command of the war. Martí drafted and the two men signed on March 25 the "Manifesto de Montecristi," which confirmed the democratic origins and the republican principles of the revolution.

Against the wishes of Gómez, who knew Martí's life was too valuable to the revolution and the future of Cuba to risk unnecessarily, Martí embarked with him and five others for Cuba, arriving by rowboat at night at Playitas, Oriente Province, on April 11. On May 6, Martí and Gómez rendezvoused at "La Mejorana" with General Antonio Maceo, who had also lent his crucial support to the revolution.

On May 19, 1895, in one of the first actions of the war, José Martí was killed in maiden combat at Dos Ríos, Oriente Province, as he prophesied in verse XXIII of *Versos sencillos*.

Another prophesy would be fulfilled in the course of the next century: "My poetry will grow, and I too will grow under the grass."

Manuel A. Tellechea

Prólogo

Mis amigos saben cómo se me salieron estos versos del corazón. Fue aquel invierno de angustia, en que por ignorancia, o por fe fanática, o por miedo, o por cortesía, se reunieron en Washington, bajo el águila temible, los pueblos hispanoamericanos. ¿Cuál de nosotros ha olvidado aquel escudo, el escudo en que el águila de Monterrey y de Chapultepec, el águila de López y de Walker, apretaba en sus garras los pabellones todos de la América? Y la agonía en que viví, hasta que pude confirmar la cautela y el brío de nuestros pueblos; y el horror y vergüenza en que me tuvo el temor legítimo de que pudiéramos los cubanos, con manos parricidas, ayudar el plan insensato de apartar a Cuba, para bien único de un nuevo amo disimulado, de la patria que la reclama y en ella se completa, de la patria hispanoamericana, —me quitaron las fuerzas mermadas por dolores injustos. Me echó el médico al monte: corrían arroyos, y se cerraban las nubes: escribí versos. A veces ruge el mar, y revienta la ola, en la noche negra, contra las rocas del castillo ensangrentado: a veces susurra la abeja, merodeando entre las flores.

¿Por qué se publica esta sencillez, escrita como jugando, y no mis encrespados VERSOS LIBRES, mis endecasílabos hirsutos, nacidos de grandes miedos, o de grandes esperanzas,

Prologue

My friends know how these verses came from my heart. It was in that winter of despair, when due to ignorance, or fanatical faith, or fear, or courtesy, the nations of Latin America met in Washington, under the fearful eagle. Who among us has forgotten that shield, a shield on which the eagle of Monterrey and Chapultepec, the eagle of López and Walker, clutched the flags of all the nations of America in its talons! Nor shall I forget the agony in which I lived, until I could confirm the energy and discretion of our people; nor the horror and shame in which I was kept by the legitimate fear that we Cubans might, with parricidal hands and solely to benefit a new concealed master, assist the senseless plan to separate Cuba from the greater Hispanic fatherland that claimed her for its own and could not be complete without her—such preoccupations sapped what strength was not consumed by unjust sorrows. The doctor sent me off to the mountains: there streams ran, clouds closed-in upon clouds, and I wrote poetry. At times the sea roars in the dark of the night, and its waves break against the stones of a bloodied castle; and at other times, a bee is humming as it forages among the flowers.

Why publish something so simple, playfully written, and not my windswept FREE VERSE, my hirsute hendecasyllables, born of great fears or great hopes, of the indomitable

o de indómito amor de libertad, o de amor doloroso a la hermosura, como riachuelo de oro natural, que va entre arena y aguas turbias y raíces, o como hierro caldeado, que silba y chispea, o como surtidores candentes? ¿Y mis VERSOS CUBANOS, tan llenos de enojo, que están mejor donde no se les ve? ¿Y tanto pecado mío escondido, y tanta prueba ingenua y rebelde de literatura? ¿Ni a qué exhibir ahora, con ocasión de estas flores silvestres, un curso de mi poética, y decir por qué repito un consonante de propósito, o los gradúo y agrupo de modo que vayan por la vista y el oído al sentimiento, o salto por ellos, cuando no pide rimas ni soporta repujos la idea tumultuosa? Se imprimen estos versos porque el afecto con que los acogieron, en una noche de poesía y amistad, algunas almas buenas, los ha hecho ya públicos. Y porque amo la sencillez, y creo en la necesidad de poner el sentimiento en formas llanas y sinceras.

José Martí   Nueva York: 1891.

love of liberty, or of the painful love of beauty, which flows as a rivulet of pure gold amid sand, turbid waters and roots, or as molten iron hissing and shooting off sparks, or as a burning fountain. Or my CUBAN VERSE, so filled with anger that it is best left where it cannot be seen? And all those hidden sins of mine, and all those ingenuous and rebellious examples of literature from my pen? And why make the publication of these wildflowers the occasion for a course on my poetics, or explain why I repeat rhymes on purpose, or classify and group them so that they reach the sentiments by sight and sound, or dispense with them altogether, when a tumultuous idea does not require rhyme or tolerate too many hammer blows! These verses are published because the affection with which they were received by some good souls, during a night of poetry and friendship, has already made them public. And because I love simplicity, and believe in the necessity of putting feelings in plain and sincere forms.

José Martí   New York: 1891.

I

Yo soy un hombre sincero
De donde crece la palma,
Y antes de morirme quiero
Echar mis versos del alma.

Yo vengo de todas partes,
Y hacia todas partes voy:
Arte soy entre las artes,
En los montes, monte soy.

Yo sé los nombres extraños
De las yerbas y las flores,
Y de mortales engaños,
Y de sublimes dolores.

Yo he visto en la noche oscura
Llover sobre mi cabeza
Los rayos de lumbre pura
De la divina belleza.

Alas nacer vi en los hombros
De las mujeres hermosas:
Y salir de los escombros
Volando las mariposas.

He visto vivir a un hombre
Con el puñal al costado,
Sin decir jamás el nombre
De aquella que lo ha matado.

1

A sincere man am I
From the land where palm trees grow,
And I want before I die
My soul's verses to bestow.

I'm a traveler to all parts,
And a newcomer to none;
I am art among the arts,
With the mountains I am one.

I know the strange names of willows,
And can tell flowers with skill:
I know of lies that can kill,
And I know of sublime sorrows.

I have seen through dead of night
Upon my head softly fall,
Rays formed of the purest light
From beauty celestial.

I have seen wings that were surging
From beautiful women's shoulders,
And seen butterflies emerging
From the refuse heap that moulders.

I have known a man to live
With a dagger at his side,
And never once the name give
Of she by whose hand he died.

Rápida, como un reflejo,
Dos veces vi el alma, dos:
Cuando murió el pobre viejo,
Cuando ella me dijo adiós.

Temblé una vez,—en la reja,
A la entrada de la viña,—
Cuando la bárbara abeja
Picó en la frente a mi niña.

Gocé una vez, de tal suerte
Que gocé cual nunca:—cuando
La sentencia de mi muerte
Leyó el alcaide llorando.

Oigo un suspiro, a través
De las tierras y la mar,
Y no es un suspiro,—es
Que mi hijo va a despertar.

Si dicen que del joyero
Tome la joya mejor,
Tomo a un amigo sincero
Y pongo a un lado el amor.

Yo he visto al águila herida
Volar al azul sereno,
Y morir en su guarida
La víbora del veneno.

Twice, for an instant, did I
My soul's reflection descried,
Twice: when my poor father died,
And when she bade me good-bye.

I trembled once, when I flung
The vineyard gate, and to my dread,
The dastard hornet had stung
My little girl on the forehead.

Such great luck to me once came
As no man would dare to envy,
When in tears my jailer read me
The death warrant with my name.

I hear a sigh across the earth,
I hear a sigh over the deep:
It is no sigh reaching my hearth,
But my son waking from sleep.

If they say I have obtained
The pick of the jeweller's trove,
A good friend is all I've gained,
And I have put aside love.

I have seen an eagle gliding,
Though wounded, across the skies;
I know the cubby where lies
The snake of its venom dying.

Yo sé bien que cuando el mundo
Cede, lívido, al descanso,
Sobre el silencio profundo
Murmura el arroyo manso.

Yo he puesto la mano osada,
De horror y júbilo yerta,
Sobre la estrella apagada
Que cayó frente a mi puerta.

Oculto en mi pecho bravo
La pena que me lo hiere:
El hijo de un pueblo esclavo
Vive por él, calla, y muere.

Todo es hermoso y constante,
Todo es música y razón,
Y todo, como el diamante,
Antes que luz es carbón.

Yo sé que el necio se entierra
Con gran lujo y con gran llanto,—
Y que no hay fruta en la tierra
Como la del camposanto.

Callo, y entiendo, y me quito
La pompa del rimador:
Cuelgo de un árbol marchito
Mi muceta de doctor.

I know that the world is weak
And must soon fall to the ground,
And, then, midst the quiet profound
The gentle brook will speak.

While trembling with joy and dread,
I have touched with hand so bold
A once-bright star that fell dead
From heaven at my threshold.

I have hid in my brave heart
The most terrible of pains,
The son of a land in chains
Lives for it and dies apart.

All is beautiful and right,
All is as music and reason;
And as diamonds ere their season,
All is coal before it's light.

I know when fools are laid to rest
Honor and tears will abound,
And that of all fruits, the best
Is left to rot in holy ground.

Without a word, I've understood
And put aside the pompous muse;
From a withered branch, I choose
To hang my doctoral hood.

II

Yo sé de Egipto y Nigricia,
Y de Persia y Xenophonte;
Y prefiero la caricia
Del aire fresco del monte.

Yo sé de las historias viejas
Del hombre y de sus rencillas;
Y prefiero las abejas
Volando en las campanillas.

Yo sé del canto del viento
En las ramas vocingleras:
Nadie me diga que miento,
Que lo prefiero de veras.

Yo sé de un gamo aterrado
Que vuelve al redil, y expira,—
Y de un corazón cansado
Que muere oscuro y sin ira.

II

I know of Egypt and Niger,
Of Persia and Xenophon, no less,
But more than these I prefer
The fresh mountain air's caress.

I know the ancient histories
Of man and his struggles for power,
But I prefer the buzzing bees
That hover round the bellflower.

I know the sound the wind made
When through the boughs it was flying:
Let no one tell me I'm lying,
There is no song as well played.

I know of a frightened fawn
That seeks the fold to expire,
And of a heart weary-worn
That dies hidden without ire.

III

Odio la máscara y vicio
Del corredor de mi hotel:
Me vuelvo al manso bullicio
De mi monte de laurel.

Con los pobres de la tierra
Quiero yo mi suerte echar:
El arroyo de la sierra
Me complace más que el mar.

Denle al vano el oro tierno
Que arde y brilla en el crisol:
A mí denme el bosque eterno
Cuando rompe en él el sol.

Yo he visto el oro hecho tierra
Barbullendo en la redoma:
Prefiero estar en la sierra
Cuando vuela una paloma.

Busca el obispo de España
Pilares para su altar;
¡En mi templo, en la montaña,
El álamo es el pilar!

Y la alfombra es puro helecho,
Y los muros abedul,
Y la luz viene del techo,
Del techo de cielo azul.

III

The pretense and vice I spurn
Of the hallway of my inn:
To my laurel hill I turn
Preferring its gentle din.

With the earth's poor everywhere,
I shall cast my lot: to me
Far more contentment is there
In mountain brook than in sea.

To the vain the gold that's softest
In crucible burning bright,
Give me the eternal forest
When the sun first shines its light.

I have seen gold to dross change
As the bubbling test tube roars;
I prefer the mountain range,
While a dove above it soars.

The sightless bishop of Spain
Wants pillars to hold his altar,
In my temple, on the mountain,
My pillars are made of poplar!

Of purest fern are the carpets
And the walls are of birch tree,
And a brilliant light it gets
From a sky-blue canopy.

El obispo, por la noche,
Sale, despacio, a cantar:
Monta, callado, en su coche,
Que es la piña de un pinar.

Las jacas de su carroza
Son dos pájaros azules:
Y canta el aire y retoza,
Y cantan los abedules.

Duermo en mi cama de roca
Mi sueño dulce y profundo:
Roza una abeja mi boca
Y crece en mi cuerpo el mundo.

Brillan las grandes molduras
Al fuego de la mañana,
Que tiñe las colgaduras
De rosa, violeta y grana.

El clarín, solo en el monte,
Canta al primer arrebol:
La gasa del horizonte
Prende, de un aliento, el sol.

¡Díganle al obispo ciego,
Al viejo obispo de España
Que venga, que venga luego,
A mi templo, a la montaña!

At night the bishop is gone
To sing his heart out in praise,
He mounts quietly his chaise,
Which is made of a pinecone.

The tiny steeds that pull his coach
Are two bluebirds taking wing;
The birch trees ring at his approach,
With the joyful airs they sing.

On a bed of stone I lay me,
Dreaming dreams sweet and profound,
At my mouth a bee flies round
And the world grows in my body.

Brilliant are the mossy moldings
As the fire of morn grows,
Dyed like the richest wall hangings,
In violet, scarlet and rose.

The songbird's notes, in hills alone,
Warn of the first red clouds to show,
And the sun with just one blow
Burns the gauze off the horizon.

Go tell the sightless prelate,
The aged bishop of Spain,
That I his visit await
To my temple on the mountain!

IV

Yo visitaré anhelante
Los rincones donde a solas
Estuvimos yo y mi amante
Retozando con las olas.

Solos los dos estuvimos,
Solos, con la compañía
De dos pájaros que vimos
Meterse en la gruta umbría.

Y ella, clavando los ojos,
En la pareja ligera,
Deshizo los lirios rojos
Que le dio la jardinera.

La madreselva olorosa
Cogió con sus manos ella,
Y una madama graciosa,
Y un jazmín como una estrella.

Yo quise, diestro y galán,
Abrirle su quitasol;
Y ella me dijo: "¡Qué afán!
¡Si hoy me gusta ver el sol!"

"Nunca más altos he visto
Estos nobles robledales:
Aquí debe estar el Cristo,
Porque están las catedrales."

IV

I will visit longingly
All the places where unseen,
My lover and I have been
Playing with waves by the sea.

The two of us were alone
Except for the company
Of twain birds that we could see
Had to the dark cavern flown.

And she her eyes riveted
On the pair as light as air,
Plucked a spray of iris red
The gardener gave to her.

The sweet honeysuckle rose
She then gathered from the dell,
And a graceful mademoiselle
Where the starlike jasmine grows.

I, the gallant beau, begun
To open her parasol;
And she said: "Don't think me droll,
Today I want to see the sun!"

"I've never seen spires as tall
As the clustered oaks appear:
Surely, the Christ must be here,
Because here is his cathedral."

"Ya sé dónde ha de venir
Mi niña a la comunión;
De blanco la he de vestir
Con un gran sombrero alón."

Después, del calor al peso,
Entramos por el camino,
Y nos dábamos un beso
En cuanto sonaba un trino.

¡Volveré, cual quien no existe,
Al lago mudo y helado:
Clavaré la quilla triste:
Posaré el remo callado!

"I know now the place that's best
For my daughter's first communion;
All in white she will be dressed,
With a hat curved like a pinion."

At dusk the light we would miss,
And on the path we'd set out,
My lover and I would kiss
Whenever a trill let out.

As one who can no longer feel,
The quiet, frozen lake I'll tour;
There shall I bury the sad keel,
And there lay down the stilled oar!

V

Si ves un monte de espumas
Es mi verso lo que ves:
Mi verso es un monte, y es
Un abanico de plumas.

Mi verso es como un puñal
Que por el puño echa flor:
Mi verso es un surtidor
Que da un agua de coral.

Mi verso es de un verde claro
Y de un carmín encendido:
Mi verso es un ciervo herido
Que busca en el monte amparo.

Mi verso al valiente agrada:
Mi verso, breve y sincero,
Es del vigor del acero
Con que se funde la espada.

V

If you've seen a mount of sea foam,
It is my verse you have seen:
My verse a mountain has been,
And a feathered fan become.

My verse is like a dagger
At whose hilt a flower grows,
My verse is a fount which flows
With a sparkling coral water.

My verse is a gentle green
And also a flaming red,
My verse is a deer wounded
Seeking forest cover unseen.

My verse is brief and sincere,
And to the brave will appeal:
With all the strength of the steel
With which the sword will appear.

VI

Si quieren que de este mundo
Lleve una memoria grata,
Llevaré, padre profundo,
Tu cabellera de plata.

Si quieren, por gran favor,
Que lleve más, llevaré
La copia que hizo el pintor
De la hermana que adoré.

Si quieren que a la otra vida
Me lleve todo un tesoro,
¡Llevo la trenza escondida
Que guardo en mi caja de oro!

VI

If I a pleasant keepsake
On leaving this world may bear,
Father profound, I would take
A lock of your silver hair.

If allowed for mercy's sake,
One more favor to implore:
The painter's portrait I'd take
Of the sister I adore.

Could I to a treasure cling
From this life in that foretold,
The hidden tresses I'd bring
I keep in a chest of gold!

VII

Para Aragón, en España,
Tengo yo en mi corazón
Un lugar todo Aragón,
Franco, fiero, fiel, sin saña.

Si quiere un tonto saber
Por qué lo tengo, le digo
Que allí tuve un buen amigo,
Que allí quise a una mujer.

Allá, en la vega florida,
La de la heroica defensa,
Por mantener lo que piensa
Juega la gente la vida.

Y si un alcalde lo aprieta
O lo enoja un rey cazurro,
Calza la manta el baturro
Y muere con su escopeta.

Quiero a la tierra amarilla
Que baña el Ebro lodoso:
Quiero el Pilar azuloso
De Lanuza y de Padilla.

Estimo a quien de un revés
Echa por tierra a un tirano:
Lo estimo, si es un cubano;
Lo estimo, si aragonés.

VII

For brave Aragon, in Spain,
I have a place in my heart
Which of Aragon's a part—
Frank, fierce, faithful, without stain.

If a fool can't comprehend
Why this is so, I'll explain:
That there I met a good friend,
And a woman's love did gain.

There on the flowery plain
Where the brave once took the field,
The people their creed maintain
If their lives they have to yield.

Should him the mayor reprimand,
Or a surly king provoke,
He wraps himself in his cloak
And dies with shotgun in hand.

I love that yellow land whose shore
The murky Ebro caressed,
The Virgin of the Pillar blessed
By martyred heroes of yore.

I esteem him who would seize
A tyrant and lay him low,
Honor to the tyrant's foe,
Cuban or Aragonese!

Amo los patios sombríos
Con escaleras bordadas;
Amo las naves calladas
Y los conventos vacíos.

Amo la tierra florida,
Musulmana o española,
Donde rompió su corola
La poca flor de mi vida.

I love its courtyards in the shade,
By winding staircases bound;
I love the naves without a sound
And vacant convents time evade.

I love that land with flowers strewn,
Whether of Spaniard or Moor,
For there the flower so poor
Of my own life came to bloom.

VIII

Yo tengo un amigo muerto
Que suele venirme a ver:
Mi amigo se sienta, y canta;
Canta en voz que ha de doler.

"En un ave de dos alas
"Bogo por el cielo azul:
"Un ala del ave es negra,
"Otra de oro Caribú.

"El corazón es un loco
"Que no sabe de un color:
"O es su amor de dos colores,
"O dice que no es amor.

"Hay una loca más fiera
"Que el corazón infeliz:
"La que le chupó la sangre
"Y se echó luego a reír.

"Corazón que lleva rota
"El ancla fiel del hogar,
"Va como barca perdida,
"Que no sabe a dónde va".

En cuanto llega a esta angustia
Rompe el muerto a maldecir:
Le amanso el cráneo: lo acuesto:
Acuesto el muerto a dormir.

VIII

I have a dead friend who lately
Has begun to visit me:
My friend sits down and sings to me,
Sings to me so dolefully:

"Upon the double-winged bird's back
I am rowing through skies of blue:
One of the bird's wings is black,
The other, gold of Cariboo."

"The heart's a madman that abhors
One color as one too few:
Either its love is two colors,
Or else it is not love's hue."

"There's a madwoman more savage
Than is the unhappy heart:
She that sucks the blood in rage,
And then a-laughing would start."

"A heart that has lost forever
The steadfast anchor of home,
Sails like a ship in foul weather,
And knows not to go or come."

If his anguish should betray him,
The dead man will curse and weep:
I pat his skull and I lay him,
Lay the dead man down to sleep.

IX

Quiero, a la sombra de un ala,
Contar este cuento en flor:
La niña de Guatemala,
La que se murió de amor.

Eran de lirios los ramos,
Y las orlas de reseda
Y de jazmín: la enterramos
En una caja de seda.

...Ella dio al desmemoriado
Una almohadilla de olor:
Él volvió, volvió casado:
Ella se murió de amor.

Iban cargándola en andas
Obispos y embajadores:
Detrás iba el pueblo en tandas,
Todo cargado de flores.

...Ella, por volverlo a ver,
Salió a verlo al mirador:
Él volvió con su mujer:
Ella se murió de amor.

Como de bronce candente
Al beso de despedida
Era su frente ¡la frente
Que más he amado en mi vida!

IX

By a spread wing, on the grove,
A tale blooms in the nightshade:
Of a Guatemalan maid,
She who lost her life to love.

The wreaths with lilies were twined,
And trimmed with henna and jasmine:
And she was laid in her coffin,
Which all in satin was lined.

...A cushion filled with a sweet spray,
She gave her forgetful lover:
He returned wed to another:
And dead of her love she lay.

She was borne in state to her grave
By ambassadors and churchmen:
And behind, with flowers laden,
Came the poor, wave upon wave.

...She opened her lattice door,
To see him again she sighed:
She saw him pass with his bride:
And then she saw him no more.

Her forehead was bronze ablaze
When I last kissed her good-bye:
Hers was the forehead that I
Have most loved in all my days!

...Se entró de tarde en el río,
La sacó muerta el doctor:
Dicen que murió de frío:
Yo sé que murió de amor.

Allí, en la bóveda helada,
La pusieron en dos bancos:
Besé su mano afilada,
Besé sus zapatos blancos.

Callado, al oscurecer,
Me llamó el enterrador:
¡Nunca más he vuelto a ver
A la que murió de amor!

...One night she entered the river,
There the doctor found her dead:
She died of a cold, they said:
I know it was love that killed her.

In the frozen sepulcher
She was placed upon a stand:
And I kissed her slender hand,
And I kissed her white slipper.

There I stood till dusk, when soft
The gatekeeper called to me:
Never again would I see
She who lost her life to love!

X

El alma trémula y sola
Padece al anochecer:
Hay baile; vamos a ver
La bailarina española.

Han hecho bien en quitar
El banderón de la acera;
Porque si está la bandera,
No sé, yo no puedo entrar.

Ya llega la bailarina:
Soberbia y pálida llega:
¿Cómo dicen que es gallega?
Pues dicen mal: es divina.

Lleva un sombrero torero
Y una capa carmesí:
¡Lo mismo que un alelí
Que se pusiese un sombrero!

Se ve, de paso, la ceja,
Ceja de mora traidora:
Y la mirada, de mora:
Y como nieve la oreja.

Preludian, bajan la luz,
Y sale en bata y mantón,
La virgen de la Asunción
Bailando un baile andaluz.

X

My soul tremulous and lonely
At nightfall will grow forlorn:
There's a show, let us go see
The Spanish dancer perform.

It is well they've taken down
The flag that stood at the entrance;
For I don't think I could go hence
If that banner were still flown.

The Spanish dancer enters then,
Looking so proud and so pale:
"From Galicia does she hail?"
No, they are wrong: she's from heaven.

She wears the matador's tricorne
And also his crimson cape:
A gilliflower to drape
And with a great hat adorn!

On passing her eyebrows show,
Eyebrows of a traitorous Moor:
And the Moor's proud look she wore,
And her ear was white as snow.

The music starts, the lights dim,
In shawl and gown, there advances
The Virgin of the Assumption
Dancing Andalucian dances.

Alza, retando, la frente;
Crúzase al hombro la manta:
En arco el brazo levanta:
Mueve despacio el pie ardiente.

Repica con los tacones
El tablado zalamera,
Como si la tabla fuera
Tablado de corazones.

Y va el convite creciendo
En las llamas de los ojos,
Y el manto de flecos rojos
Se va en el aire meciendo.

Súbito, de un salto arranca:
Húrtase, se quiebra, gira:
Abre en dos la cachemira,
Ofrece la bata blanca.

El cuerpo cede y ondea;
La boca abierta provoca;
Es una rosa la boca:
Lentamente taconea.

Recoge, de un débil giro,
El manto de flecos rojos:
Se va, cerrando los ojos,
Se va, como en un suspiro...

Baila muy bien la española;
Es blanco y rojo el mantón:
¡Vuelve, fosca, a su rincón
El alma trémula y sola!

Her head raised in challenge, she
The cape o'er her shoulders will spread:
With her arched arms framing her head,
She taps her foot ardently.

Her studied taps tear the batten,
As if each heel were a blade,
And the stage had been inlaid
With the broken hearts of men.

The festive feeling is burning
In the fire of her eyes,
The red-speckled shawl now flies
In the air as she is turning.

With a sudden leap she starts,
Rebounds, then turns, and bows down:
Wide her cashmere shawl she parts
To offer us her white gown.

All her body yields and sways;
Her open mouth is enticing;
A rose is her mouth: while dancing
She's tapping her heels always.

Then turns she feebly to wind
The long and red-speckled shawl:
And shutting her eyes to all,
In a sigh leaves all behind.

The Spanish dancer has done well;
Red and white was her long shawl:
The tremulous, lonely soul
Withdraws again to its cell!

XI

Yo tengo un paje muy fiel
Que me cuida y que me gruñe,
Y al salir, me limpia y bruñe
Mi corona de laurel.

Yo tengo un paje ejemplar
Que no come, que no duerme,
Y que se acurruca a verme
Trabajar, y sollozar.

Salgo, y el vil se desliza
Y en mi bolsillo aparece;
Vuelvo, y el terco me ofrece
Una taza de ceniza.

Si duermo, al rayar el día
Se sienta junto a mi cama:
Si escribo, sangre derrama
Mi paje en la escribanía.

Mi paje, hombre de respeto,
Al andar castañetea:
Hiela mi paje, y chispea:
Mi paje es un esqueleto.

XI

I have a page of loyal-renown
Who bends to all my desires,
Takes care of me, never tires,
Cleans and shines my laurel crown.

My page excels at his job:
He will neither eat nor sleep,
And writhes in pain when I keep
Long hours at work, or sob.

When I leave, the scoundrel dashes
And in my pocket appears;
When I return, the dolt nears
To offer a cup of ashes.

When I wake at crack of dawn,
He's up and beside my bed;
When I write, the blood he's shed
Into my inkwell is drawn.

My page I can always count on,
Though he rattles as he walks,
Chills and warms the one he stalks:
My page is a skeleton.

XII

En el bote iba remando
Por el lago seductor,
Con el sol que era oro puro
Y en el alma más de un sol.

Y a mis pies vi de repente,
Ofendido del hedor,
Un pez muerto, un pez hediondo
En el bote remador.

XII

Once I was sailing for fun
On a lake of great allure,
Like gold the sun shone so pure,
And my soul more than the sun.

Then suddenly I could smell
Before I saw at my feet,
A foul fish, with death replete,
At the bottom of the well.

XIII

Por donde abunda la malva
Y da el camino un rodeo,
Iba un ángel de paseo
Con una cabeza calva.

Del castañar por la zona
La pareja se perdía:
La calva resplandecía
Lo mismo que una corona.

Sonaba el hacha en lo espeso
Y cruzó un ave volando:
Pero no se sabe cuándo
Se dieron el primer beso.

Era rubio el ángel; era
El de la calva radiosa,
Como el tronco a que amorosa
Se prende la enredadera.

XIII

Where the holly's overspread
And the straight road takes a bend,
An angel and a bald head
Together their way had wend.

By the chestnut grove, the pair
Were finally lost from sight:
But the bald head shone from there
As bright as a crown of light.

The ax was heard in the forest,
The soaring bird was not missed:
But none the knowledge possessed
Of when the two had first kissed.

The angel was blonde; and he,
Of the resplendent bald head,
The trunk was which lovingly
The clinging vine overspread.

XIV

Yo no puedo olvidar nunca
La mañanita de otoño
En que le salió un retoño
A la pobre rama trunca.

La mañanita en que, en vano,
Junto a la estufa apagada,
Una niña enamorada
Le tendió al viejo la mano.

XIV

Ne'er will I forget, I vow,
That Fall morning long ago,
When I saw a new leaf grow
Upon the old withered bough.

That dear morning when for naught,
By a stove whose flame had died,
A girl in love stood beside
An old man, and his hand sought.

XV

Vino el médico amarillo
A darme su medicina,
Con una mano cetrina
Y la otra mano al bolsillo:
¡Yo tengo allá en un rincón
Un médico que no manca
Con una mano muy blanca
Y otra mano al corazón!

Viene, de blusa y casquete,
El grave del repostero,
A preguntarme si quiero
O Málaga o Pajarete:
¡Díganle a la repostera
Que ha tanto tiempo no he visto,
Que me tenga un beso listo
Al entrar la primavera!

XV

The yellow doctor comes yet
To give me his remedy,
With one jaundiced hand for me
And the other in his pocket.
In a corner dwells apart
A doctor whose touch is light,
With a hand so very white
And the other on his heart!

The pastry chef comes to me
In his paper hat and smock,
To ask I sample his stock
Of Málaga or sherry.
Please inform the pastrycook,
She I've longed to see and miss,
To prepare for me a kiss
And for Spring's first sign to look!

XVI

En el alféizar calado
De la ventana moruna,
Pálido como la luna,
Medita un enamorado.

Pálida, en su canapé
De seda tórtola y roja,
Eva, callada, deshoja
Una violeta en el té.

XVI

Opening the moorish grate
To lean upon the wet sill,
Pale as the moon, and so still,
A lover ponders his fate.

Pale, beneath her canopy
Of red silk and turtledove,
Eve, who says nothing of love,
A violet plucks in her tea.

XVII

Es rubia: el cabello suelto
Da más luz al ojo moro:
Voy, desde entonces, envuelto
En un torbellino de oro.

La abeja estival que zumba
Más ágil por la flor nueva,
No dice, como antes, "tumba":
"Eva" dice: todo es "Eva".

Bajo, en lo oscuro, al temido
Raudal de la catarata:
¡Y brilla el iris, tendido
Sobre las hojas de plata!

Miro, ceñudo, la agreste
Pompa del monte irritado:
¡Y en el alma azul celeste
Brota un jacinto rosado!

Voy, por el bosque, a paseo
A la laguna vecina:
Y entre las ramas la veo,
Y por el agua camina.

La serpiente del jardín
Silba, escupe, y se resbala
Por su agujero: el clarín
Me tiende, trinando, el ala.

¡Arpa soy, salterio soy
Donde vibra el Universo:
Vengo del sol, y al sol voy:
Soy el amor: soy el verso!

XVII

She's blonde: her loose hair behold,
Which sets off her Moorish eyes:
Since I saw her, my heart lies
Trapped in that whirlwind of gold.

The eager summer bee will cleave
To new flowers all the more fast;
It says not "tomb," as in the past:
It says "Eve," and all is Eve.

Amid the gloom, I will drop
To the fearful cataract:
A rainbow shines through the black,
Above the silver tree-top!

Awestruck, I gaze at the wild
Splendor of the nettled hill:
In my sky-blue soul beguiled
There blooms a pink daffodil!

Through the forest I am tracking,
Bound for the lagoon nearby:
When through the branches, I spy
Her upon the waters walking.

The snake of the garden, hissing,
Spits and slithers to its hole:
The songbird pouring its soul
Is stretching to me its wing.

I am the harp and psalterion
Where vibrates the universe:
I come and go to the sun:
I am love: and I am verse!

XVIII

El alfiler de Eva loca
Es hecho del oro oscuro
Que le sacó un hombre puro
Del corazón de una roca.

Un pájaro tentador
Le trajo en el pico ayer
Un relumbrante alfiler
De pasta y de similor.

Eva se prendió al oscuro
Talle el diamante embustero:
Y echó en el alfiletero
El alfiler de oro puro.

XVIII

The brooch that foolish Eve did own
Was sculpted of darkest gold ore,
Which once a pure man had dug for
In the very heart of a stone.

Last night a tempting bird had flown
And brought in his beak the damsel,
A brilliant brooch she could not tell
Was made of paste and of rhinestone.

Now on her shrouded waist Eve wore
The fake diamond she judged the best,
And tossed into the jewelry chest
The brooch she had of pure gold ore.

XIX

Por tus ojos encendidos
Y lo mal puesto de un broche,
Pensé que estuviste anoche
Jugando a juegos prohibidos.

Te odié por vil y alevosa:
Te odié con odio de muerte:
Náusea me daba de verte
Tan villana y tan hermosa.

Y por la esquela que vi
Sin saber cómo ni cuándo,
Sé que estuviste llorando
Toda la noche por mí.

XIX

Because your eyes were two flames
And your brooch wasn't pinned right,
I thought you had spent the night
In playing forbidden games.

Because you were vile and devious
Such deadly hatred I bore you,
To see you was to abhor you,
So lovely and yet so villainous.

Because a note came to light,
I know now where you had been,
And what you had done unseen—
Cried for me all the long night.

XX

Mi amor del aire se azora;
Eva es rubia, falsa es Eva:
Viene una nube, y se lleva
Mi amor que gime y que llora.

Se lleva mi amor que llora
Esa nube que se va:
Eva me ha sido traidora:
¡Eva me consolará!

XX

The wind my love terrifies:
Eve is blonde, but Eve is not true:
A passing cloud takes to the blue,
My love as she moans and cries.

It takes my love as she cries
The cloud that passes from view:
Eve has betrayed me anew,
Eve consoles me with her lies!

XXI

Ayer la vi en el salón
De los pintores, y ayer
Detrás de aquella mujer
Se me saltó el corazón.

Sentada en el suelo rudo
Está en el lienzo: dormido
Al pie, el esposo rendido:
Al seno el niño desnudo.

Sobre unas briznas de paja
Se ven mendrugos mondados:
Le cuelga el manto a los lados,
Lo mismo que una mortaja.

No nace en el torvo suelo
Ni una viola, ni una espiga:
¡Muy lejos, la casa amiga,
Muy triste y oscuro el cielo!...

¡Ésa es la hermosa mujer
Que me robó el corazón
En el soberbio salón
De los pintores de ayer!

XXI

Yesterday, at the art show,
I saw her, and yesterday
My heart from me flew away
After that woman to follow.

She sits on the bare ground to rest,
On canvas her vigil she keeps:
The tired spouse at her feet sleeps
And a naked babe at her breast.

Atop a bale of straw is seen
The peeled remnants of their last meal:
Her draping mantle she can feel
As if a death shroud it had been.

On the grim earth for the weary
Grow neither violet nor thorn,
From a loving home they're torn
And the sky is dark and dreary!

That lovely woman made away
With my heart and will not free it,
At the proud salon's exhibit
Of masters of yesterday!

XXII

Estoy en un baile extraño
De polaina y casaquín
Que dan, del año hacia el fin,
Los cazadores del año.

Una duquesa violeta
Va con un frac colorado:
Marca un vizconde pintado
El tiempo en la pandereta.

Y pasan las chupas rojas,
Pasan los tules de fuego,
Como delante de un ciego
Pasan volando las hojas.

XXII

I have come to the strange ball
Where tails and gaiters abound,
And the best hunters the year-round
The New Year wait to install.

A violet duchess is seen
In the arms of a red coat:
A painted viscount of note
Keeps time on a tambourine.

And the red waistcoats whirl by,
And the flaming tulles are flowing,
As dead leaves the wind is blowing
In front of a blind man's eye.

XXIII

Yo quiero salir del mundo
Por la puerta natural:
En un carro de hojas verdes
A morir me han de llevar.

No me pongan en lo oscuro
A morir como un traidor:
¡Yo soy bueno, y como bueno
Moriré de cara al sol!

XXIII

From this world I will depart,
And the natural door will try:
Green leaves will cover the cart
On which I'm taken to die.

Don't in darkness let me lie
With traitors to come undone:
I am good and as the good die,
I will die face to the sun!

XXIV

Sé de un pintor atrevido
Que sale a pintar contento
Sobre la tela del viento
Y la espuma del olvido.

Yo sé de un pintor gigante,
El de divinos colores,
Puesto a pintarle las flores
A una corbeta mercante.

Yo sé de un pobre pintor
Que mira el agua al pintar,—
El agua ronca del mar,—
Con un entrañable amor.

XXIV

A daring painter I know
Who goes to paint happily,
On the wind's canvas to sow
The foam of obscurity.

A great painter here abides
Who paints with colors divine,
But must his genius confine
To painting flowers on shipsides.

I know a poor painter who stares
At the sea while he is painting—
At the waves raging and fainting—
With the deep love that he bears.

XXV

Yo pienso, cuando me alegro
Como un escolar sencillo,
En el canario amarillo,—
¡Que tiene el ojo tan negro!

Yo quiero, cuando me muera,
Sin patria, pero sin amo,
Tener en mi losa un ramo
De flores,—¡y una bandera!

XXV

I am still taken aback
With a simple schoolboy's glee
By the yellow canary,
Whose eye is so very black!

When I die without a country,
Nor to any man a slave,
I want a wreath on my grave
And a flag draped over me!

XXVI

Yo que vivo, aunque me he muerto,
Soy un gran descubridor,
Porque anoche he descubierto
La medicina de amor.

Cuando al peso de la cruz
El hombre morir resuelve,
Sale a hacer bien, lo hace, y vuelve
Como de un baño de luz.

XXVI

I who live though I have died,
Claim a great discovery,
For last night I verified
Love is the best remedy.

When weighed by the cross, a man
Resolves to die for the right;
He does all the good he can
And returns bathed in the light.

XXVII

El enemigo brutal
Nos pone fuego a la casa:
El sable la calle arrasa,
A la luna tropical.

Pocos salieron ilesos
Del sable del español:
La calle, al salir el sol,
Era un reguero de sesos.

Pasa, entre balas, un coche:
Entran, llorando, a una muerta:
Llama una mano a la puerta
En lo negro de la noche.

No hay bala que no taladre
El portón: y la mujer
Que llama, me ha dado el ser:
Me viene a buscar mi madre.

A la boca de la muerte,
Los valientes habaneros
Se quitaron los sombreros
Ante la matrona fuerte.

Y después que nos besamos
Como dos locos, me dijo:
"¡Vamos pronto, vamos, hijo:
La niña está sola: vamos!"

XXVII

The brutal enemy last night
Our houses torched as we slept:
The streets with his sword were swept,
By the tropical moonlight.

Few there were who had not bore
The Spanish sabre's wild fury:
And at sunrise all could see
The streets steeped in blood and gore.

Amid the shooting a coach in flight
A dead woman took inside:
A voice cried out, a knock defied
The leaden clamor of the night.

Bullets then were flying wildly,
And the door with holes was rife:
The woman calling gave me life:
My mother had come to get me.

Through the jaws of death she pressed on,
And the brave Havanans, in awe,
Their hats would lift when they saw
In the streets the strong-willed matron.

As madmen kiss, we kissed so,
While around us people fled;
"Quickly, let's go quickly," she said:
"The baby's alone; let's go!"

XXVIII

Por la tumba del cortijo
Donde está el padre enterrado,
Pasa el hijo, de soldado
Del invasor: pasa el hijo.

El padre, un bravo en la guerra,
Envuelto en su pabellón
Álzase: y de un bofetón
Lo tiende, muerto, por tierra.

El rayo reluce: zumba
El viento por el cortijo:
El padre recoge al hijo,
Y se lo lleva a la tumba.

XXVIII

Across the homestead on the lea,
Where in his grave the father lay,
The son, a soldier, makes his way:
The son in the invader's army.

The father, for bravery renowned,
Draped in the flag that he upheld,
Rose from the grave and his son felled
With one swift blow upon the ground.

The lightning flashes 'cross the sky,
The winds against the farmhouse beat:
Father the son lifts in defeat
And on his grave sets him to lie.

XXIX

La imagen del rey, por ley,
Lleva el papel del Estado:
El niño fue fusilado
Por los fusiles del rey.

Festejar el santo es ley
Del rey: y en la fiesta santa
¡La hermana del niño canta
Ante la imagen del rey!

XXIX

By law the king's face appears
On all the instruments of state,
And the king's own volunteers
With his guns sealed the boy's fate.

It's the law to celebrate
The sainted namesakes of kings,
And there the boy's sister sings
In front of the royal portrait!

XXX

El rayo surca, sangriento,
El lóbrego nubarrón:
Echa el barco, ciento a ciento,
Los negros por el portón.

El viento, fiero, quebraba
Los almácigos copudos:
Andaba la hilera, andaba,
De los esclavos desnudos.

El temporal sacudía
Los barracones henchidos:
Una madre con su cría
Pasaba, dando alaridos.

Rojo, como en el desierto,
Salió el sol al horizonte:
Y alumbró a un esclavo muerto,
Colgado a un seibo del monte.

Un niño lo vio: tembló
De pasión por los que gimen:
¡Y, al pie del muerto, juró
Lavar con su vida el crimen!

XXX

The lightning the heaven scorches,
And the clouds are bloodstained patches:
The ship its hundreds disgorges
Of captive blacks through the hatches.

The fierce winds and brutal rains
Beat against the dense plantation:
In a file the slaves in chains
Are led naked for inspection.

All the storm's fury assails
The thatched huts swollen with slaves:
A harried mother bewails
The human litter none saves.

Red as in the desert zone,
The sun rose on the horizon:
And upon the dead slave shone,
Hanged from a tree on the mountain.

A boy saw him there and shook
With passion for the oppressed:
And at his feet an oath took
That this crime would be redressed.

XXXI

Para modelo de un dios
El pintor lo envió a pedir:—
¡Para eso no! ¡para ir,
Patria, a servirte los dos!

Bien estará en la pintura
El hijo que amo y bendigo:—
¡Mejor en la ceja oscura,
Cara a cara al enemigo!

Es rubio, es fuerte, es garzón
De nobleza natural:
¡Hijo, por la luz natal!
¡Hijo, por el pabellón!

Vamos, pues, hijo viril:
Vamos los dos: si yo muero,
Me besas: si tú... ¡prefiero
Verte muerto a verte vil!

XXXI

The painter wanted a model
That he could pose for a god:
Not for that was he begot
But to go with me to battle!

There he would pose to advantage,
The son I bless and love so:
Better here, on the cliff's edge,
Face to face with charging foe!

He is blonde, and strong and manly,
With natural nobility:
My son, because born to me,
And because born to my country!

Let us go, my brave son, while
We may both go; if I die,
Kiss me; if you, fain would I
See you dead than know you vile!

XXXII

En el negro callejón
Donde en tinieblas paseo,
Alzo los ojos, y veo
La iglesia, erguida, a un rincón.

¿Será misterio? ¿Será
Revelación y poder?
¿Será, rodilla, el deber
De postrarse? ¿Qué será?

Tiembla la noche: en la parra
Muerde el gusano el retoño;
Grazna, llamando al otoño,
La hueca y hosca cigarra.

Graznan dos: atento al dúo
Alzo los ojos, y veo
Que la iglesia del paseo
Tiene la forma de un búho.

XXXII

In the black and narrow alley
Where I stroll as shadows fall,
I look up and there can see
The corner church standing tall.

Could it be a mystery,
A power or revelation,
Or is it an obligation
That would make me bend my knee?

The night quivers: on the grapevine
The worm is eating its fill:
The cicada, dark and shrill,
Calls out for Autumn's first sign.

While listening to the yowl,
I look up and there can see
The corner church by the alley
Is in the shape of an owl.

XXXIII

De mi desdicha espantosa
Siento, oh estrellas, que muero:
Yo quiero vivir, yo quiero
Ver a una mujer hermosa.

El cabello, como un casco,
Le corona el rostro bello:
Brilla su negro cabello
Como un sable de Damasco.

¿Aquélla?... Pues pon la hiel
Del mundo entero en un haz,
Y tállala en cuerpo, y ¡haz
Un alma entera de hiel!

¿Ésta?... Pues esta infeliz
Lleva escarpines rosados,
Y los labios colorados,
Y la cara de barniz.

El alma lúgubre grita:
"¡Mujer, maldita mujer!"
¡No sé yo quién pueda ser
Entre las dos la maldita!

XXXIII

I'm so frightfully unhappy,
I feel, oh stars, I could die!
I want to live, I want to see
A lovely woman pass by.

Like a helmet, her headdress
A beautiful face protects,
Her black hair the light reflects
As the sword of Damascus.

What of that one? Well, find all
The world's gall, and then enmesh,
Cover it in so much flesh,
And you have a soul that's all gall!

Well, this one? Such a disgrace!
The creature red slippers wears,
Paints her lips red if she cares,
And puts on a barnished face.

The sorrowful soul then screamed:
"Damn you, woman, twice damn you!"
I know not which of the two
The more accursed should be deemed!

XXXIV

¡Penas! ¿quién osa decir
Que tengo yo penas? Luego,
Después del rayo, y del fuego,
Tendré tiempo de sufrir.

Yo sé de un pesar profundo
Entre las penas sin nombres:
¡La esclavitud de los hombres
Es la gran pena del mundo!

Hay montes, y hay que subir
Los monte altos; ¡después
Veremos, alma, quién es
Quien te me ha puesto al morir!

XXXIV

Who dares the assumption make
That I have sorrows to tend?
When lightning and fire end,
The time to grieve I will take.

Of all the sorrows I could name
The most profound is unspoken:
To hold and keep in slavery men
Is the world's terrible shame.

There are mountains still to climb,
And climb tall mountains we must;
Later, my soul, we'll see just
Who planned your death in my prime!

XXXV

   ¿Qué importa que tu puñal
Se me clave en el riñón?
¡Tengo mis versos, que son
Más fuertes que tu puñal!

   ¿Qué importa que este dolor
Seque el mar, y nuble el cielo?
El verso, dulce consuelo,
Nace alado del dolor.

XXXVI

   Ya sé: de carne se puede
Hacer una flor: se puede,
Con el poder del cariño,
Hacer un cielo,—¡y un niño!

   De carne se hace también
El alacrán; y también
El gusano de la rosa,
Y la lechuza espantosa.

XXXV

What matters that your dagger
Into my heart is plunged far?
I have my verses which are
More powerful than your dagger!

What matters that this great pain
Clouds the sky, and drains the sea?
My verse, sweet solace to me,
Is born with the wings of pain.

XXXVI

The uses of flesh are mild:
Of flesh one can make a flower,
And of flesh can with love's power
Make a heaven and a child!

The uses of flesh are foul:
Of flesh the scorpion is made,
The worm that makes the rose fade,
As well as the frightening owl.

XXXVII

Aquí está el pecho, mujer,
Que ya sé que lo herirás;
¡Más grande debiera ser,
Para que lo hirieses más!

Porque noto, alma torcida,
Que en mi pecho milagroso,
Mientras más honda la herida,
Es mi canto más hermoso.

XXXVII

Here, woman, my heart you see,
Wound it, as I know you will;
It should all the bigger be
That you might wound it more still!

For, twisted soul, I have found
In my miraculous heart,
While more deeper is the wound
The more beautiful the art.

XXXVIII

¿Del tirano? Del tirano
Di todo, ¡di más!: y clava
Con furia de mano esclava
Sobre su oprobio al tirano.

¿Del error? Pues del error
Di el antro, di las veredas
Oscuras: di cuanto puedas
Del tirano y del error.

¿De mujer? Pues puede ser
Que mueras de su mordida;
¡Pero no empañes tu vida
Diciendo mal de mujer!

XXXVIII

Of tyrants? Well, say of tyrants
All there's to say, more, then brand
With the rage of a slave's hand,
Brand on such the shame of tyrants.

Of error? Well, say of error
What's in cavern and dark winding,
Say all the horror you're finding
Of the tyrant and of error.

Of women? Well, then of women,
Though of their bite you may die,
Do not your life vilify
By saying ill word of women!

XXXIX

Cultivo una rosa blanca,
En julio como en enero,
Para el amigo sincero
Que me da su mano franca.
Y para el cruel que me arranca
El corazón con que vivo,
Cardo ni oruga cultivo:
Cultivo una rosa blanca.

XXXIX

I have a white rose to tend
In July as in January;
I give it to the true friend
Who offers his frank hand to me.
And to the cruel one whose blows
Break the heart by which I live,
Thistle nor thorn do I give:
For him, too, I have a white rose.

XL

Pinta mi amigo el pintor
Sus angelones dorados,
En nubes arrodillados,
Con soles alrededor.

Pínteme con sus pinceles
Los angelitos medrosos
Que me trajeron, piadosos,
Sus dos ramos de claveles.

XL

My friend the artist portrays
His angels golden and stout,
Kneeling on clouds as they pray,
With bursting suns all about.

Paint me with your best creations
The angels, small and afraid,
Who the thoughtful present made
To me of their red carnations.

XLI

Cuando me vino el honor
De la tierra generosa,
No pensé en Blanca ni en Rosa
Ni en lo grande del favor.

Pensé en el pobre artillero
Que está en la tumba, callado:
Pensé en mi padre, el soldado:
Pensé en mi padre, el obrero.

Cuando llegó la pomposa
Carta, en su noble cubierta,
Pensé en la tumba desierta,
No pensé en Blanca ni en Rosa.

XLI

When I the honor was brought
A kind land on me bestowed,
Of Blanche nor of Rose I thought,
Nor of the favor I owed.

I thought then of an old soldier,
Who lies silent, with his Maker:
Of my poor father, the worker,
Of my poor father, the soldier.

When I the pompous letter got,
Written in the noble script,
I thought of the lonely crypt,
Of Blanche and Rose I thought not.

XLII

En el extraño bazar
Del amor, junto a la mar,
La perla triste y sin par
Le tocó por suerte a Agar.

Agar, de tanto tenerla
Al pecho, de tanto verla
Agar, llegó a aborrecerla:
Majó, tiró al mar la perla.

Y cuando Agar, venenosa
De inútil furia, y llorosa,
Pidió al mar la perla hermosa,
Dijo la mar borrascosa:

"¿Qué hiciste, torpe, qué hiciste
De la perla que tuviste?
La majaste, me la diste:
Yo guardo la perla triste".

XLII

Wandering through love's strange bazaar,
Held by the seaside, not far,
A sad pearl bright as a star
By great luck fell to Agar.

Too long to her breast she pressed it,
And too long her eyes caressed it,
That soon she came to detest it
And dropped it as the sea crested.

The venomous Agar crying,
Into a great rage then flying,
From the sea the pearl tried prying,
With the stormy sea replying:

"What did you, fool, without regard
To the fairest pearl in the world?
Back to my depths the pearl you hurled,
Now the sad pearl you spurned I guard."

XLIII

Mucho, señora, daría
Por tender sobre tu espalda
Tu caballera bravía,
Tu cabellera de gualda:
  Despacio la tendería,
  Callado la besaría.

Por sobre la oreja fina
Baja lujoso el cabello,
Lo mismo que una cortina
Que se levanta hacia el cuello.
  La oreja es obra divina
  De porcelana de China.

Mucho, señora, te diera
Por desenredar el nudo
De tu roja cabellera
Sobre tu cuello desnudo:
  Muy despacio la esparciera,
  Hilo por hilo la abriera.

XLIII

Much, my lady, I should dare
If down your back I could drape,
Drape your wild hair from the nape,
Let fall your golden-red hair.
Slowly would I let it fall
And silently kiss it all.

Over the delicate ears
Luxuriously falls the hair,
Like a curtain in mid-air,
Which at the nape disappears.
Her ear was divinely made
Of the rarest Chinese jade.

Much, my lady, I should dare
To undo the knot that holds it,
Holds your red hair and enfolds it,
So it fall over the nape bare.
I would part it with great care,
Part it slowly, hair by hair.

XLIV

Tiene el leopardo un abrigo
En su monte seco y pardo:
Yo tengo más que el leopardo,
Porque tengo un buen amigo.

Duerme, como en un juguete,
La mushma en su cojinete
De arce del Japón: yo digo:
"No hay cojín como un amigo".

Tiene el conde su abolengo:
Tiene la aurora el mendigo:
Tiene ala el ave: ¡yo tengo
Allá en México un amigo!

Tiene el señor presidente
Un jardín con una fuente,
Y un tesoro en oro y trigo:
Tengo más, tengo un amigo.

XLIV

The leopard has found its den
In the forest, brown and dry,
More than the leopard have I,
A good friend's the best haven.

As on a toy, she lies to rest
The geisha on the maple cushion:
I also rest and can attest,
"A friend is like no other cushion."

The Count his lineage would spend
As beggars the hope dawn brings;
But I, as the birds have wings,
In Mexico have a friend!

The President, they contend,
Has a garden with a fountain,
And rich stores of gold and grain:
I have more, I have a friend.

XLV

Sueño con claustros de mármol
Donde en silencio divino
Los héroes, de pie, reposan:
¡De noche, a la luz del alma,
Hablo con ellos: de noche!
Están en fila: paseo
Entre las filas: las manos
De piedra les beso: abren
Los ojos de piedra: mueven
Los labios de piedra: tiemblan
Las barbas de piedra: empuñan
La espada de piedra: lloran:
¡Vibra la espada en la vaina!:
Mudo, les beso la mano.

¡Hablo con ellos, de noche!
Están en fila: paseo
Entre las filas: lloroso
Me abrazo a un mármol: "¡Oh mármol,
Dicen que beben tus hijos
Su propia sangre en las copas
Venenosas de sus dueños!
¡Que hablan la lengua podrida
De sus rufianes! ¡que comen
Juntos el pan del oprobio,
En la mesa ensangrentada!
¡Que pierden en lengua inútil
El último fuego!: ¡dicen,
Oh mármol, mármol dormido,
Que ya se ha muerto tu raza!"

XLV

I dream of marble cloisters
Where in silence blessed
The standing heroes rest:
At night, by the soul's light,
I speak to them: at night!
They are on file: I pass
Among their ranks: I kiss
Their hands of stone: they open
Their eyes of stone: they move
Their lips of stone: they shake
Their beards of stone: they grasp
Their swords of stone: and weep:
The swords spin in their sheaths!:
Silent, I kiss their hands.

I speak to them at night!
They are on file: I pass
Among the ranks: and weeping too,
Embrace a statue: "Oh, statue,
It's said that your sons drink
The blood of their own veins
In their masters' poisoned cups!
That they speak the foul tongue
Of ruffians! and with them
Eat the bread of opprobrium
At the bloodstained table!
And lose in useless words
Their last fire! It's said,
Oh statue, sleeping statue,
That your race is dead!"

Échame en tierra de un bote
El héroe que abrazo: me ase
Del cuello: barre la tierra
Con mi cabeza: levanta
El brazo, ¡el brazo le luce

Lo mismo que un sol!: resuena
La piedra: buscan el cinto
Las manos blancas: del soclo
Saltan los hombres de mármol!

The hero I embraced
Flings himself at me:
He grabs me by the collar:
Sweeps the earth with my head:
And raising his sunlike arm,
The statue speaks: the white hands
Reach for their belts:
And from their pedestals
The men of marble leap!

XLVI

Vierte, corazón, tu pena
Donde no se llegue a ver,
Por soberbia, y por no ser
Motivo de pena ajena.

Yo te quiero, verso amigo,
Porque cuando siento el pecho
Ya muy cargado y deshecho,
Parto la carga contigo.

Tú me sufres, tú aposentas
En tu regazo amoroso,
Todo mi amor doloroso,
Todas mis ansias y afrentas.

Tú, porque yo pueda en calma
Amar y hacer bien, consientes
En enturbiar tus corrientes
Con cuanto me agobia el alma.

Tú, porque yo cruce fiero
La tierra, y sin odio, y puro,
Te arrastras, pálido y duro,
Mi amoroso compañero.

Mi vida así se encamina
Al cielo limpia y serena,
Y tú me cargas mi pena
Con tu paciencia divina.

XLVI

Your sorrows, my heart, you should hide
Where no man can e'er discover,
So that you may spare my pride,
Don't trouble with them another.

I love you, Verse, my friend true,
Because when in pieces torn
My heart's too burdened, you've borne
All my sorrows upon you.

For me you suffer and bear
Upon your amorous lap
The painful love I leave there,
Every anguish, every slap.

As I love, in peace with all,
And do good works, as my goal,
You thrash your waves, rise and fall,
With whatever weighs my soul.

That I may cross with fierce stride,
Pure and without hate, this vale,
You drag yourself, hard and pale,
The loving friend at my side.

And so my life its way will wend
To the sky serene and pure,
While you my sorrows endure
And with divine patience tend.

Y porque mi cruel costumbre
De echarme en ti te desvía
De tu dichosa armonía
Y natural mansedumbre;

Porque mis penas arrojo
Sobre tu seno, y lo azotan,
Y tu corriente alborotan,
Y acá lívido, allá rojo,

Blanco allá como la muerte,
Ora arremetes y ruges,
Ora con el peso crujes
De un dolor más que tú fuerte,

¿Habré, como me aconseja
Un corazón mal nacido,
De dejar en el olvido
A aquel que nunca me deja?

¡Verso, nos hablan de un Dios
Adonde van los difuntos:
Verso, o nos condenan juntos,
O nos salvamos los dos!

Because I know this cruel habit
Of throwing myself on you,
Upsets your harmony true
And tries your gentle spirit.

Because on your breast I've shed
All of my sorrows and torments,
And have whipped your quiet currents,
Which are here white and there red,

And then pale as death become,
At once roaring and attacking,
And then beneath the weight cracking
Of pain it can't overcome.

Should I the advice have taken
Of a heart so misbegotten,
Would have me leave you forgotten,
Who never me has forsaken?

Verse, they tell us of One Greater
To whom the dying appealed;
Verse, as one our fates are sealed:
We are damned or saved together!